ULTIMATE SUPERCARS

McLAREN 12C

By Carrie Myers

Kaleidoscope
Minneapolis, MN

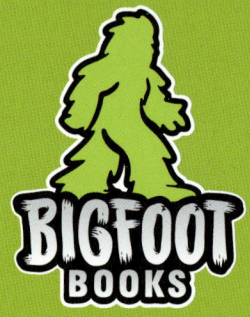

The Quest for Discovery Never Ends

....

This edition is co-published by agreement between Kaleidoscope and World Book, Inc.

Kaleidoscope Publishing, Inc.
6012 Blue Circle Drive
Minnetonka, MN 55343 U.S.A.

World Book, Inc.
180 North LaSalle St., Suite 900
Chicago IL 60601 U.S.A.

All rights reserved. No part of this book may be reproduced in any form without written permission from the publishers.

Kaleidoscope ISBNs
978-1-64519-031-8 (library bound)
978-1-64494-238-3 (paperback)
978-1-64519-131-5 (ebook)

World Book ISBN
978-0-7166-4332-6 (library bound)

Library of Congress Control Number
2019940247

Text copyright ©2020 by Kaleidoscope Publishing, Inc. All-Star Sports, Bigfoot Books, and associated logos are trademarks and/or registered trademarks of Kaleidoscope Publishing, Inc.

Printed in the United States of America.

FIND ME IF YOU CAN!

Bigfoot lurks within one of the images in this book. It's up to you to find him!

TABLE OF CONTENTS

Chapter 1: *A New Record* *4*

Chapter 2: *Car of the Year* *10*

Chapter 3: *Roof or No Roof?* *16*

Chapter 4: *Pure McLaren* *24*

    Beyond the Book *28*

    Research Ninja *29*

    Further Resources *30*

    Glossary *31*

    Index *32*

    Photo Credits *32*

    About the Author *32*

CHAPTER 1

A NEW RECORD

Kevin Estre tears up the track in his McLaren 12C GT3. The car revs and roars. It sounds like an angry bumblebee. Estre's McLaren is orange. It has black trim.

Kevin Estre set his record in a McLaren 12C GT3 like this one.

It's June 20, 2014. The Nürburgring race is in Germany. Gray clouds are overhead. Trees flash past. Estre only sees the track. It's the world's longest. Estre turns the steering wheel hard. The 12C GT3 whips through a tight turn.

GT3 RACES

GT3 races are for modified road cars. The cars are changed to fit the race specifications, or rules. Most drivers enter GT3 races for fun. McLaren 12C GT3s were built from 2011–2015. They won four championship races. They won sixty other races.

The 12C GT3 has a large spoiler.

Estre is alone on the track. He is taking a qualifying lap. The qualifying lap takes place before the race. Only the fastest drivers go on to race. The 12C GT3 is built with **carbon fiber**. Carbon fiber makes it light and fast. The car also has a **spoiler** and **side vents**. These make it **aerodynamic**.

Estre sets a lap time record. It's eight minutes, ten seconds. He beats the last record by over six seconds. His average speed is 116 miles per hour (186 km/hr).

FUN FACT
McLaren cars are known for their "papaya orange" color. All McLaren race cars start out this color.

Estre qualifies for the race. He will take **pole position**. This is the best starting spot. He and his 12C GT3 are off to a great start!

Estre's 12C GT3 was made for race car drivers. It's based on the 12C road car. The road car was made for anyone to drive. 12C road cars look different than Estre's car. They have much smaller spoilers. But they're still fast.

spoiler/air brake

McLaren logo

PARTS OF A
MCLAREN 12C

removable roof (on the 12C Spider)

side slits

single-hinged doors

CHAPTER 2

CAR OF THE YEAR

Bruce McLaren was born on August 30, 1937. He lived in New Zealand. When he was fifteen, he and his father rebuilt an old car. They painted it bright red. McLaren entered an uphill race. The wind whipped against his face. He smelled the sea air. The car roared to the top. McLaren won! It was the start of an incredible career.

In 1959, McLaren entered the United States Grand Prix. It was in Sebring, Florida. The day was sunny and warm.

Formula 1 cars look different from other race cars.

McLaren drove lightning-fast down the 5-mile (8-km) track. He became the youngest **Formula 1** champion to date.

But McLaren wanted more. He itched to build his own cars and have his own team. He started McLaren Racing in 1966. Today, the company has different parts. McLaren Racing builds and races Formula 1 cars. McLaren Automotive builds road cars.

The F1 was McLaren's first road car. A road car is built for anyone to drive. The F1 launched in 1992. It used new technology. It cost $1 million to make.

McLaren stopped making F1s in 1998. For thirteen years, McLaren only built race cars. Then it built the 12C. It based the car on the F1. The 12C launched in 2011.

Drivers loved the 12C. They said it was stunning. Driving it was mind-blowing. Its speed was crazy.

The F1 was designed to have the speed and handling of a Formula 1 car with the luxury of a road car.

Top Gear is a television show about supercars. The Stig is a driver for *Top Gear*. He always wears a helmet. No one sees his face. He is quite mysterious.

The Stig has tested over 150 cars. He compares their speeds. The 12C does a lap in 1 minute, 16.2 seconds. Only one other car is faster. *Top Gear* gave the 12C Spider its top award. It was its 2012 Car of the Year.

FUN FACT
McLaren cars have won more Formula 1 races than any company except Ferrari.

Vehicles are assembled by hand at the McLaren Production Center.

CHAPTER 3

ROOF OR NO ROOF?

Kihan visits a McLaren showroom. He wants to buy a used 12C. Kihan likes classic cars. He also likes rare cars. Only around 4,000 12Cs were ever made. He can choose a Coupe or a Spider. The Coupe has a regular roof.

The Spider is a convertible. Its roof can be folded back. The driver can enjoy the open air. The Coupe weighs a few pounds less than the Spider. Its top speed is 3 miles per hour (5 km/h) faster.

The McLaren 12C was made from 2011 to 2014.

FUN FACT
The design of the 12C is inspired by nature.

The 12C's doors are different than most cars. Kihan notices they don't open out. Instead, they open up. Most car doors have two hinges. The 12C's doors have only one. They take up less space when they open. Drivers can get in more easily. Kihan sees the doors don't have handles.

The McLaren 12C's doors have a single hinge. They open up, not out.

The doors sense the driver's hand. They open by themselves.

Kihan learns that 12Cs are made from carbon fiber. Everything about the 12C is extra light. This includes the tires and the paint. That's so the car will go extra fast.

Finally, Kihan takes a Spider for a test drive. He reaches the highway. He hits the gas. The 12C gathers speed. McLaren 12Cs are low to the ground and curved. They have special features to control air flow. This makes the cars go and stop faster. The **splitter** and **diffuser** move air along the 12C's bottom. The **air brake** is on the back of the car. It helps the car stop quickly. The side vents move air through the car to keep it cool.

Kihan approaches a turn. He is driving fast. He needs to slow down to make the turn. 12Cs have Brake Steer technology. They have high **torque**. These features help the 12C steer and brake around corners. The Spider brakes smoothly.

Kihan is pleased. He will buy a 12C. But he can't decide. Will he buy the Spider? Or will he buy the Coupe? It's a tough decision!

The air brake tilts up to help the car stop. It can also act as a spoiler to make the car more aerodynamic.

CUSTOM-MADE

The 12C isn't made anymore. But McLaren makes other cars. Customers can design their own car, inside and out. They choose their seat covers and the paint color. They choose the size and weight of their tires. And they can choose a convertible or a coupe!

THE MCLAREN 12C
IN DETAIL

Height: 3.9 feet (1.2 m)

Width: 6.3 feet (1.9 m)

Length: 14.8 feet (4.5 m)

COUPE COST: $241,800

Weight: 3,161 pounds (1,434 kg)

Top Speed: 207 miles per hour (333 km/h)

Time from 0–62 miles per hour (0–100 km/h): 3.1 seconds

Height: 3.9 feet (1.2 m)

Width: 6.3 feet (1.9 m)

SPIDER COST: $268,250

Length: 14.8 feet (4.5 m)

Weight: 3,249 pounds (1,474 kg)

Top Speed: 204 miles per hour (328 km/h)

Time from 0–62 miles per hour (0–100 km/h): 3.3 seconds

CHAPTER 4

PURE MCLAREN

McLaren stopped making 12Cs in 2014. It launched a new car called the 650S. That car took the 12C's place. Now, 12Cs are considered classics.

Amari owns a 12C. She drives it to work. She drives it to the grocery store. Sometimes she drives very fast! But she wants to feel like a real race car driver. Luckily, she can.

The 650S replaced the 12C.

She decides to find an experience racetrack. These racetracks let customers drive supercars.

Amari chooses a program called Pure McLaren. It is run by McLaren Automotive. Drivers can bring their own McLaren. They can also rent one.

Pure McLaren events take place all over the world. Amari considers Germany first. But she decides she wants to go to Bahrain. Bahrain is a country in the Middle East. The event is two days long.

The driving course is in the desert. The sun is hot. The air is dry. Amari's 12C is a Coupe. Its body is classic papaya orange. The 12C flashes in the sun.

Amari drives her 12C through twists. She takes sharp corners. A McLaren coach sits in the car. He gives Amari tips. She becomes a better driver. Now she feels like a real professional. Next year, Amari plans to drive her 12C in Portugal!

FUN FACT
Pure McLaren's Arctic Experience takes place north of the Arctic Circle.

Pure McLaren events let drivers learn to drive like pros.

BEYOND THE BOOK

After reading the book, it's time to think about what you learned. Try the following exercises to jumpstart your ideas.

THINK

THAT'S NEWS TO ME. Kevin Estre raced in the 2014 Nürburgring race. He drove the McLaren 12C GT3. How might news sources be able to fill in more detail about this? What new information could you find in news articles? Where could you go to find those sources?

CREATE

PRIMARY SOURCE. A primary source is an original document, photograph, or interview. Make a list of different primary sources you might be able to find about the McLaren 12C. What new information might you learn from these sources?

SHARE

SUM IT UP. Write one paragraph summarizing the important points from this book. Make sure it's in your own words. Don't just copy what is in the text. Share the paragraph with a classmate. Does your classmate have any comments about the summary? Do they have additional questions about the McLaren 12C?

GROW

REAL-LIFE RESEARCH. What places could you visit to learn more about supercars? What other things could you learn while you were there?

RESEARCH NINJA

Visit **www.ninjaresearcher.com/0318** to learn how to take your research skills and book report writing to the next level!

RESEARCH

DIGITAL LITERACY TOOLS

SEARCH LIKE A PRO
Learn about how to use search engines to find useful websites.

FACT OR FAKE?
Discover how you can tell a trusted website from an untrustworthy resource.

TEXT DETECTIVE
Explore how to zero in on the information you need most.

SHOW YOUR WORK
Research responsibly—learn how to cite sources.

WRITE

GET TO THE POINT
Learn how to express your main ideas.

PLAN OF ATTACK
Learn prewriting exercises and create an outline.

DOWNLOADABLE REPORT FORMS

FURTHER RESOURCES

BOOKS

Crane, Cody. *Race Cars*. Children's Press, 2018.

Cruz, Calvin. *McLaren 12C*. Bellwether Media, 2016.

Mason, Paul. *British Supercars: McLaren, Aston Martin, Jaguar*. PowerKids Press, 2019.

WEBSITES

Factsurfer.com gives you a safe, fun way to find more information.

1. Go to www.factsurfer.com.

2. Enter "McLaren 12C" into the search box and click 🔍.

3. Select your book cover to see a list of related websites.

GLOSSARY

aerodynamic: An aerodynamic design reduces the drag, or pull, on a car as it moves through air. The 12C's aerodynamic design helps it go faster.

air brake: An air brake pops up when the driver brakes at high speeds. The air brake is the wing on the back of the 12C.

carbon fiber: Carbon fiber is a very strong, lightweight material. Using carbon fiber to build a car makes it lighter and faster.

diffuser: A diffuser is a part that takes the air under the car and sends it out the back. There is a diffuser on the bottom and back of the 12C.

Formula 1: Formula 1 is an international form of car racing popular in Europe. Formula 1 race cars have large, wide wheels and open cockpits.

pole position: A car in pole position is in the front row on the inside of the track. Pole position is the best starting position.

side vents: The side vents are openings that allow air into the radiator. The 12C's side vents keep the car cool.

splitter: A splitter is a part on the front of the car that makes it more aerodynamic. The splitter on the 12C divides air into two streams, sending some air under the car and some on top.

spoiler: A spoiler is a wing that changes the airflow around the car. The racing 12C has a spoiler to make it more aerodynamic.

torque: Torque measures the power an engine can put out. A car with more torque will accelerate faster.

INDEX

650S, 24

air brake, 8, 20

brakes, 20

cost, 12, 22–23

doors, 9, 18–19

Estre, Kevin, 4–8

F1, 12

Formula 1, 10–11, 14

GT3, 4–8

McLaren, Bruce, 10–11

New Zealand, 10

Nürburgring Race, 4–8

papaya orange, 7, 26

Pure McLaren, 25–27

race cars, 4–8, 10–12

record, 7, 11

size, 22–23

steering, 5, 26

Top Gear, 14

top speed, 17, 22–23

PHOTO CREDITS

The images in this book are reproduced through the courtesy of: McLaren Media, front cover (car), pp. 4–5, 5, 6, 6–7, 12–13, 13, 14, 16–17, 20–21, 22, 23, 26, 26–27, 30; gyn9037/Shutterstock Images, front cover (city); Artem Kliatchkine/Shutterstock Images, p. 3; Dutourdumonde Photography/Shutterstock Images, p. 8; David Cardinez/Shutterstock Images, pp. 8–9; Abdul Razak Latif/Shutterstock Images, pp. 10–11; AP Images, p. 11; Red Line Editorial, p. 15; Steve Lagreca/Shutterstock Images, pp. 18–19; Dong liu/Shutterstock Images, pp. 24–25.

ABOUT THE AUTHOR

Carrie Myers lives in New York City with her husband, three children, and one very hairy guinea pig. She enjoys music, books, and visiting family in Hawaii. She does not enjoy washing dishes.